MAINTAINING DISCIPLINE IN CLASSROOM INSTRUCTION

Sammy Brown

Time   11:20

Days   MTWT

Room   M100F

MAINTAINING DISCIPLINE IN CLASSROOM INSTRUCTION

A Title in the CURRENT TOPICS
IN CLASSROOM INSTRUCTION Series

William J. Gnagey
Professor of Psychology
Illinois State University

Macmillan Publishing Co., Inc.
New York
Collier Macmillan Publishers,
London

Copyright © 1975, William J. Gnagey

Printed in the United States of America

All rights reserved. No part of this book may be reproduced or transmitted in any form or by any means, electronic or mechanical, including photocopying, recording, or any information storage and retrieval system, without permission in writing from the Publisher.

Macmillan Publishing Co., Inc.
866 Third Avenue, New York, New York 10022

Collier-Macmillan Canada, Ltd.

Library of Congress Cataloging in Publication Data

Gnagey, William J   (date)
   Maintaining discipline in classroom instruction.

   (Current topics in classroom instruction series)
   Bibliography: p.
   Includes index.
   1. Classroom management.   I. Title.
LB3013.G58   371.1'02   74-26843
ISBN 0-02-344160-7

Printing: 2 3 4 5 6 7 8   Year: 6 7 8 9 0

Preface

The material in this book is meant to bridge the research-implementation gap so that classroom teachers can begin immediately to improve the learning atmosphere for their students.

While a positive, humanistic, reward-centered approach pervades most of the techniques described in this book, we have not hesitated to include recent material on effective punishment.

We hope that a careful reading of this brief, straightforward presentation will help both experienced teachers and teachers in training to become more effective disciplinarians in the truest sense of the word.

William J. Gnagey
Illinois State University

Contents

Chapter

1	**Defining Classroom Discipline**	1
	Breaking the Classroom Rules	1
	Establishing a Learning Environment	1
	Preventing Classroom Misbehavior	2
	Controlling Deviants Directly	2
	Controlling Deviants by Proxy	2
	Reconditioning Student Behavior	2
	Using Punishment Constructively	3
	Increasing Self-Control	3
	Applying Glasser's Reality Therapy	3
	Evaluating Your Own Techniques	3
	Learning More About Maintaining Discipline	3
	Summary	4
2	**Preventing Classroom Misbehavior**	5
	Making Smooth Transitions	5
	Engineering Optimal Movement	6
	Keeping Students Alert and Accountable	7
	Arranging for Variety	8
	Being "With It" As a Teacher	9
	Summary	10
3	**Controlling Deviants Directly**	11
	Reducing Frustration	11
	Activating Student Motives	12
	Using Physical Force	13
	Summary	13
4	**Controlling Deviants by Proxy**	15
	Producing a Ripple Effect	15
	Clarifying Deviancy Situations	16
	Being Consistently Firm	16
	Keeping Control Task- (Not Teacher-) Centered	16
	Determining the Deviant's Effect	17
	Measuring the Effect of the Deviant's Prestige	18

vii

	Measuring the Effect of the Deviant's Response	18
	Summary	18
5	**Reconditioning Student Behavior**	19
	Using Behavior Modification	19
	Using Positive Reinforcement	19
	Using the Extinction Principle	20
	Applying Constructive Modeling	20
	Cueing Acceptable Behavior	20
	Using Negative Reinforcement	21
	Using a Token Economy	21
	Analyzing the Token Economy	22
	Summary	22
6	**Using Punishment Constructively**	23
	Avoiding Revenge	23
	Using Punishment Effectively	24
	Build Positive Relationships	25
	Punish Early and Consistently	25
	Punishment Should Be Moderately Intense	25
	Tell Students What Behavior Is Being Punished	26
	Make Acceptable Alternatives Clear and Valent	26
	Change Punishments Occasionally	26
	Summary	26
7	**Increasing Self-Control**	27
	Defining Self-Control	27
	Learning Self-Management	27
	Teaching Self-Control	28
	Punishment and Self-Control	29
	Summary	29
8	**Applying Glasser's Reality Therapy: An Ecclectic Approach**	30
	Five Basic Elements of Discipline	31
	Steps in Reality Therapy	32
	Classroom Meetings	33
	Summary	33
Appendix A:	Checklist for Evaluating Your Disciplinary Techniques	35
Appendix B:	References	38
Index		47

MAINTAINING DISCIPLINE IN CLASSROOM INSTRUCTION

Chapter 1
Defining Classroom Discipline

Regardless of the tons of articles that have been written on the subject (see Appendix B), classroom discipline continues to be a major problem for many school teachers.

Since opinions about classroom control vary widely, we have made two previous efforts (Gnagey, 1965; Gnagey, 1968) to apply the results of bona fide research to this knotty problem.

This book updates and broadens these two previous efforts and focuses on material that can be clearly described and applied to authentic classroom situations.

Breaking the Classroom Rules

It is assumed that misbehavior occurs whenever a student breaks one of the classroom rules. These rules are so different from classroom to classroom that it is impossible to construct a set of guidelines that would be acceptable in all or even most situations.

Earlier (Gnagey, 1968), we pointed out that most lists of classroom rules are based on moral, personal, legal, safety and educational considerations. We also suggested that lists of rules should be minimal, relevant, meaningful and positive.

Establishing a Learning Environment

While this book does not ignore the other bases, it assumes that the major reason for "good classroom discipline" is to maintain an environment that will optimize appropriate learning.

In order to maximize the chances that this book will help you solve some of your own discipline problems, we have written seven chapters, each drawing on a slightly different body of research. It will soon become obvious that there is some overlap among the several approaches. This should be quite reassuring since it increases the credibility of the repeated principles and suggests that classroom discipline can be based upon firmer ground than professional opinion.

Preventing Classroom Misbehavior

Chapter 2 is based upon a series of fine research studies carried out under the direction of Jacob S. Kounin (1970) at Wayne State University. The results clearly described a number of classroom management techniques that prevent many disciplinary episodes from ever happening.

Controlling Deviants Directly

Chapter 3 draws heavily from the clinical research of Fritz Redl and David Wineman (1957), and William W. Wattenberg (1959). The control techniques that are described in this section are considered "antiseptic" since they achieve control without debilitating side effects.

Controlling Deviants by Proxy

In Chapter 4, the "ripple effect" investigations of Kounin (1958) and his associates form the basis for specific suggestions about gaining control over an entire class by successfully disciplining one of its leaders. This discussion adds new dimensions to the old principle of "making an example" of a student who has misbehaved.

Reconditioning Student Behavior

In Chapter 5, behavior modification is brought to bear on classroom discipline. Five important principles of behavior change are explained and applied to typical classroom deviancies. Examples range from simple use of the Premack Principle (Grandma's Rule) to the establishment of a token economy.

Using Punishment Constructively

Chapter 6 takes a new look at the use of punishment in the classroom. Both abrasive and deprivative measures are discussed along with the side effects on the learning process. Instead of ignoring punishment altogether or relegating it to the position of an odious last resort, this section details ways in which punishment may be made more effective in increasing constructive classroom control.

Increasing Self-Control

The research of Justin Aronfreed (1965) and others forms the basis for Chapter 7. Two divergent schools of thought on self-control are compared with a view to teaching students to behave themselves while the teacher is not present. Since one is based on reward and the other on punishment, you should be able to choose one that fits your own disciplinary needs and philosophy of education.

Applying Glasser's Reality Therapy

The last chapter presents a brief description of William Glasser's (1969) therapeutic approach to classroom discipline. It is a system that involves a whole school setting and, therefore, requires a great deal of cooperation between administration and staff. You will also find that many of the suggestions in this section are congruent with principles that have emerged in previous chapters. This is the only chapter, however, that describes the use of classroom meetings to improve the disciplinary problems for the whole class.

Evaluating Your Own Techniques

Appendix A serves as both a review and an evaluation device. Conscientious attention to this checklist should help you discover your disciplinary strengths and weaknesses so that you can improve your own ability to maintain a relatively trouble-free learning environment for your students.

Learning More About Maintaining Discipline

Appendix B provides a recent and extensive bibliography of articles and books about classroom discipline. A few older references are included because they are basic to the understanding of the more recent treatments.

Since most of the titles are descriptive, you should be able to find additional information on almost any specialized aspect of discipline that interests you.

SUMMARY

This book updates and broadens the author's earlier books on maintaining classroom discipline. It assumes that a discipline problem occurs when a rule of the classroom is broken and that the goal of effective discipline is an environment that facilitates appropriate learning.

The book presents seven slightly different approaches to classroom control, most of which are based on a substantial body of research.

At the end of the volume, an evaluative checklist and a comprehensive bibliography help teachers to assess their disciplinary strengths and weaknesses and delve more deeply into control problems that have a special interest for them.

Chapter 2
Preventing Classroom Misbehavior

"Let's all put away our arithmetic books and get out our social studies texts," smiled Miss Jensen. "We're going to see if we can answer the questions over chapter four."

The fourth graders at Eagleton School followed the familiar directions quietly and were almost ready to work when Miss Jensen abruptly backtracked, "By the way, who can tell me why we had to borrow in that last subtraction problem?" Eagleton's heretofore docile fourth graders began to squirm visibly. Several began whispering to each other. Miss Jensen finally had to raise her voice before things settled down again.

Do you know what happened? Would you have predicted the change? What could Miss Jensen have done to prevent the misbehavior that ensued?

In an attempt to answer questions like these, Jacob Kounin painstakingly analyzed hundreds of hours of videotape records of self-contained elementary classrooms (Kounin, 1970). He found that students were more involved in their learning activities and were less likely to misbehave when their teachers were skilled in maintaining smoothness, optimal lesson movement, group focus, and high interest.

Making Smooth Transitions

Students are more likely to be involved and well behaved if transitions are smooth instead of jerky. Many teachers have learned to get their pupils ready for such changes by announcing them well in advance of the actual switch. Mr. Brownlee accomplishes this by announcing, "You should finish up your spelling practice in about three minutes so we can get started on our new social studies chapter."

The posting of (and adhering to) a daily schedule adds to smoothness because everyone knows when the transitions will occur and there are no unexpected switches. If students participate in the schedule-making procedure, it can be even more effective in keeping the transitions smooth.

There are a number of management mistakes which may destroy the smoothness of a learning sequence, thereby inhibiting lesson involvement and increasing misbehavior. Stimulus-boundedness, thrusts, dangles, truncations and flip-flops are a few that are cited by Kounin.

A *stimulus-bounded* teacher often "gets off the track" of the lesson by reacting to other, relatively unimportant things that are going on at the same time. In the middle of a recitation on the parts of the human eye, Mrs. Joslin interjects, "John, if you don't sit up straight, your back will grow crooked." Regardless of the truth of her statement, the lesson jerks to a momentary halt and the smoothness is lost.

A similar management mistake is called a *thrust*. This comes about when a teacher suddenly "butts in" to the learning situation with some announcement irrelevant to the stimuli in the classroom. As her chemistry class was working on a test, Miss Court broke in unexpectedly, "I just remembered that Monday is Washington's birthday and there will be no school." Certainly the announcement could have been saved until after the tests were passed in so that the smoothness could be preserved.

Dangles also disrupt smoothness. Mr. Bunt had just taken some time to arouse interest in a new piece of scientific equipment he was about to demonstrate. Remembering that he hadn't passed back Friday's quiz, he proceeded to do so with comments about certain difficult questions. When all the papers had been returned, he walked back to the front of the room to resume his demonstration.

When one learning activity is begun, only to be left in suspended animation for a time while other matters are attended to, smoothness is destroyed. If the teacher never does return to the initial subject, a *truncation* has been committed.

The mistake that Miss Jensen made in the opening episode of this chapter was a *flip-flop*. In any transition where one activity is terminated and another begun, going back to the supposedly "finished" lesson disrupts the smoothness visibly.

Engineering Optimal Movement

When a lesson moves along fast enough to be interesting, students tend to be better behaved and to become more involved in the learning experience. Kounin divides management errors which slow down this momentum into two categories— overdwelling and fragmentation.

Behavior overdwelling refers to excessive nagging, preaching or moralizing about things pupils have done. Students often refer to this as "making a federal case out of it." Whenever a teacher ascends the soap box in response to a minor deviancy, an unnecessary slowdown occurs.

Actone overdwelling consists of spending an inordinate amount of time on a small part of a complex behavior. During a penmanship period, a teacher might spend a third of the time emphasizing the correct posture when it is obvious to the students. Since they already know how to sit, this actone overdwelling constitutes an unnecessary slowdown.

When a teacher overemphasizes a learning tool to the exclusion of the objective of the learning activity, *prop overdwelling* occurs. Sometimes the proper passing out of workbooks becomes an end in itself rather than a means of learning. This may cause another unnecessary slowdown.

There are some teachers who take an inordinate amount of time giving directions when their students are already familiar with the task and anxious to get on with it. Kounin calls this slowdown *task overdwelling*.

Group fragmentation is a slowdown which involves having individuals do one at a time what is usually a group activity, such as lining up for lunch. Mr. Johnson wants all his pupils to be sitting quietly at their seats before he allows them to line up. He then looks for "straight sitters" and chooses one at a time to line up. This certainly slows down the pace of the transition.

Prop or actone fragmentation refers to the unnecessary splitting up of the parts of any coordinated action. Mrs. Hensen's English class know the parts of a sonnet and have written several. Each time, however, Mrs. Hensen goes through an explanation of the octave, the sestet and the couplet, asking for examples of each. This slows down lesson momentum unnecessarily when all she would have needed to say was, "Tonight I want you all to write another Spencerian sonnet."

Keeping Students Alert and Accountable

Kounin's videotape study also revealed a relationship between a teacher's skill in keeping pupils alert and accountable, and their work involvement and freedom from deviancy.

In recitation sessions, teachers may create some *suspense* before calling upon a reciter. "I'm searching for a person who looks like he knows the answer. Let me see...."

Picking reciters randomly also keeps students on their toes, while pre-establishing the order of recitation inhibits group alertness. Perhaps you can remember a foreign language class in which each person took his turn translating a paragraph aloud. Since the recitations always followed the seating order, you could count up and find which one yours would be and then ignore the other paragraphs.

Interspersing *mass unison* responses such as, "Let's see the hands of everyone who thinks Jill's answer is correct," is an effective group alerting device. It has the added advantage of evoking responses from shy pupils who are afraid of solo performances.

Some teachers call upon listening children to detect or *respond to mistakes* that the reciter makes. This makes it necessary for each child to listen to and evaluate each recitation. After getting an answer from one pupil, some teachers immediately ask another, "Do you agree with that answer?" If the second student merely answers "yes" or "no," the effective teacher counters with, "Why do you think so?"

Presenting unusual material in novel ways keeps the class group focused on the lesson, while the mundane and the usual produce boredom. Mr. Sand teaches the Civil War by dividing students into Yanks and Rebs who debate the issues which finally resulted in the war. Students read the history text with high interest so they can perform well in the debate.

Similar to those cues which keep students alert and focused upon the lesson are those which demand *accountability*. Techniques which hold children responsible for their learning performances increase their task involvement and decrease their rates of misbehavor.

Teachers often ask children to hold up their productions for inspection. Mrs. English provides her students with a set of numerals so they can hold up their answers to arithmetic problems. In this way, each child is held accountable for his work.

Classes in foreign languages are often asked to recite words and phrases in unison while the teacher listens for mistakes. Each student in this way is held accountable for his pronunciation. Modern language laboratories use sophisticated electronic equipment to do the same job.

Whenever students are asked to *demonstrate* their skills and knowledge so that the teacher and others may check up on them, accountability results.

Mrs. Spielman gives a math quiz every week. To help students get ready for this, she explains certain types of problems and assigns practice exercises which include the answers. She doesn't have to correct homework because each student knows he will be called upon to demonstrate his skill in the quiz.

Arranging for Variety

The results of Kounin's study also revealed a relationship between lesson variety and student behavior. Although there was no apparent relationship in the recitation settings, variety in seatwork correlated significantly with both work involvement and low deviancy rates. There were several kinds of variety that were observed.

Variety in content is probably easier to achieve in a self-contained classroom since so many different subjects are taught there. It is more of a challenge for the high school teacher to bring in from other areas materials that are relevant to the topic.

Another aspect of variety is the *covert behavior mode* required by the learning activities. This is accomplished by providing tasks which run the gamut from simple memorization to critical problem-solving, thereby requiring a variety of levels of intellectual challenge.

Using a number of different *presentation patterns* adds lesson variety. Even a format which initially works beautifully becomes boring when used continually. The use of learning games is often a welcome and profitable variation.

The creative use of a variety of learning *props* adds interest to the classroom. Newspapers, slides, movies and tape recorders are just a few that have been used to advantage.

Many teachers use a variety of *group configurations* in their learning activities. Sometimes the entire class listens to a presentation, while other lessons involve small interacting groups. At other times, a class may be split down the middle for "spelling bee" type activities.

Effective teachers also provide variety in the type of *responsibility* they place on students. While some assignments may be detailed and demanding, others allow students to choose their own topics and develop their own methods of presentation.

The *overt behavior mode* must also be varied if interest is to be maintained. Writing, reading, presenting, drawing, constructing, standing, sitting, moving: all these are better mixed and rotated so that one mode is not overused.

Variety can also be increased by varying the geographic *location* of activities in a class. Sitting in fastened down seats facing the same walls day after day can be deadening.

Being "With It" As A Teacher

Perhaps you can remember having a teacher who had "eyes in the back of his head." Perhaps you *are* one. If so, Kounin would say that you are "withit." Any teacher who demonstrates to her pupils that she knows what's going on has lots of "withitness."

Specifically, the withit teacher disciplines the right deviant rather than someone else in the vicinity of the turmoil. A high school language teacher was the butt of much teenage ridicule because he never seemed to know who was causing trouble in class. Bedlam would often break out behind his back as he wrote laboriously on the chalk board. At the peak of the noise, he would swing around, spin-the-bottle fashion, and point at whichever student lined up with his index finger. "You—go to the principal's office." But his students were very philosophical about it all. They said that since they all misbehaved in his class every day, that this random way of locating a culprit averaged out pretty well so that a few students didn't have to suffer unfairly from his lack of "withitness."

Withit teachers also stop major deviancies rather than attending to minor ones that are occurring concurrently. If a class clown is about to disrupt the whole group, the "withit" teacher ignores the two girls whispering in the back row and rings down the curtain on the clown's act.

Because the withit teacher knows what is going on, he/she acts promptly to use control techniques that will stop the misbehaviors. Waiting until after class to reprimand a student for being impolite is quite ineffective since he's forgotten the context of his misbehavior. His impertinence should be dealt with immediately.

Classrooms where the pupil work involvement is high and where misbehavior rates are low often have teachers who can handle two or more *overlapping situations* simultaneously without losing contact with any of them. If the teacher is helping a small group work on a project, he can answer the questions of another student without ignoring either the group or the student.

SUMMARY

Jacob S. Kounin's videotape study showed that there are a number of managerial techniques which are associated with students who have high learning activity involvement and low deviancy rates. The following principles should help you apply these findings.

1. Make your transitions smooth and avoid mistakes involving stimulus-boundedness, thrusts, dangles, truncations and flip-flops.
2. Keep your lessons moving right along and avoid unnecessary slowdowns involving either overdwelling or fragmentation.
3. Keep your students alert by using suspense, random recitation, mass unison responses, recitation evaluation, and presentation of unusual materials.
4. Make your students accountable for their learning performances by requiring production inspection, unison recitation monitoring, and skill demonstration.
5. Keep your lessons interesting by introducing variety in all aspects of your classroom operation.
6. Pay close attention to the behavior of your students so that you can discipline the right deviants, act promptly, and control major deviancies.
7. When you are called upon to handle overlapping situations, be sure to alternate your attention between both constantly.

As you increase your skill in these managerial techniques, your students will become more involved in their lessons and engage in fewer misbehaviors.

Chapter 3
Controlling Deviants Directly

Although it would be nice if all disciplinary problems could be prevented, even the most proficient classroom managers must expect to deal with some misbehavior episodes daily.

Even if the classroom rules are clear and academic frustration is kept to a minimum, many deviant acts occur because of situations outside school which are beyond the teacher's control. Some students have learned behaviors at home that conflict with the standards set at school (Kvareceus, 1945). Others are just mimicking deviant adult models (Kagan, 1958). Still others are displacing upon the teacher and other students negative feelings which they have learned in previous situations (Gnagey, 1968).

Some other recent studies (Srivastava, 1972; Brody *et al.*, 1973) have established relationships between student personality traits and their record of misbehavior in school. Certainly the teacher cannot be held responsible for the early formation of student personality traits.

But one must develop techniques that will control such deviancies, regardless of their source. In fact, exemplary control techniques must not only curb the misbehavior but should also inhibit contagion, maintain good human relations, cause learning to become more efficient and cause students to want to learn more (Gnagey, 1968, p. 32-34).

Reducing Frustration

Whenever students cannot reach their goals, frustration results. Many students react to frustration by becoming hostile and aggressive, thus creating discipline problems. Whenever a control technique helps a student move closer to his goals, frustration is reduced and much hostility-based misbehavior disappears in the bargain. It is probable that the effectiveness of optimal lesson movement in Chapter 2 is based upon the elimination of frustration caused by slowdowns.

Hurdle help (Redl and Wattenberg, 1959) may be the most effective way to control misbehaviors based upon academic frustration. When a student is given some assistance in mastering his assignments, he not only has a reduced need to be aggressive, but it gives his self-concept a lift when he finally understands the problem material.

Restructuring the situation (Redl and Wattenberg, 1959) is another control technique based upon frustration reduction. Sometimes teachers can sense that they just aren't getting through and that even students who are trying can't seem to understand the concepts and principles in the lesson. At this point, the creative teacher scraps his or her plan and takes another approach. When his students finally "get the point," their misbehavior rate decreases. This is another place where learning games can often come to the rescue.

Temptation removal (Redl and Wineman, 1957) is another technique which reduces frustration. When there are attractive stimuli in the classroom which divert student attention from their lessons, learning becomes just that much harder. Pulling the shades to shut out a playground ballgame removes a whole set of interesting stimuli that might frustrate classroom goals.

Establishing routines for taking care of pencil sharpening, lining up, lavatory-going, and such daily necessities is another way of reducing frustration. Sydney Cellar (1951) found that teachers with well-behaved classes had a well organized set of procedures for such things. Using a clearly defined lavatory pass system makes uncomfortable waiting unnecessary and avoids embarrassing accidents.

Practice alerts like fire and disaster drills are excellent ways to forestall frustrating and dangerous reactions to emergency situations. Previewing field trips before the fact performs the same function.

Once frustration-produced tension has built up, *laugh therapy* is sometimes beneficial. When the teacher tells a "funny" during a time of high frustration, he often "brings the house down" with students laughing "until the tears come." This undeserved applause is a signal that a lot of tension was already there, just waiting to burst forth. Laughter is an acceptable way to drain off the results of frustration.

Activating Student Motives

In most schools, most students want to "behave" most of the time. If this were not true, it would be next to impossible to have anything but chaos in the classroom. There are a series of control techniques that merely "touch off" the good intentions that students already have.

Visual signals are often enough to get errant students back on the track. The finger-to-lip signal is quickly recognized as "be quiet" and can be implemented without the oral reprimand that might distract students who are already on the academic target.

One creative teacher used red and green cards to control misbehavior. As long as the green card was up, the students knew that all signals were go. When things began to move toward chaos, a red signal was an effective reminder that a malfunction had occurred and needed repair.

Interest recharging may be necessary when students forget their goals momentarily and get to "horsing around." Teachers can often remind the deviants of their goals and the importance of their behavior. Sometimes a question like, "How many pages have you finished?" is enough to motivate students to get back to work.

Explaining cause and effect relationships between a student's behavior and its probable results will stimulate an appropriate switch from deviancy to approved behavior. Swimming instructors often show how running on the pool deck can lead to serious injury. Shop teachers sometimes show how improper use of a power tool can result in a severed finger.

Sometimes a *post mortem* discussion of "what went wrong" can help students see cause and effect after the fact. When the dynamics of the situation are finally understood, similar situations can be avoided in the future.

Using Physical Force

All of the previous techniques we have described have been relatively nonviolent in nature. While we deal more fully with punishment in Chapter 6, there are times when a student must be forcibly restrained in order to protect him and the other students around him.

This *protective restraint* is usually applied when a student has an uncontrolled tantrum and lashes out at others. At times like these, a teacher must often become a sort of human strait jacket for the disturbed pupil until he has spent his energy and is no longer dangerous. Obviously this is only possible when the student is enough smaller to make this possible.

SUMMARY

Since some deviancies will occur regardless of a teacher's excellence in classroom management, he/she must learn some techniques to respond to misbehavior.

In order to reduce student frustration, a teacher should:

1. Help students master difficult skills and concepts.
2. Switch to new teaching approaches when old ones aren't doing the job.
3. Remove from the classroom as many distractions as possible.
4. Establish effective routines for taking care of daily chores.
5. Practice emergency procedures so they will go smoothly if needed.
6. Help students laugh off their frustrations when tension is high.

In order to help usually well-behaved students recover from momentary lapses into misbehavior, a teacher may:

1. Develop visual signals to restore order.
2. Ask questions that remind students of their goals.
3. Help students understand the probable effects of their misbehavior.

In order to protect students from being hurt, a teacher may occasionally need to physically restrain an actively aggressive pupil.

Chapter 4
Controlling Deviants by Proxy

"Oh no you don't, Henry Weber," shouted Miss Linders, "you stay right where you are. I'm going to make an example of you!"

Henry had been caught in the act of throwing erasers when Miss Linders was out of the room. He stood there transfixed with an eraser still clutched in his hand.

Miss Linders advanced toward the culprit, ruler in hand. "Stick out your hands, Henry Weber, hurry up!"

Henry closed his eyes while the angry teacher stung his knuckles several times with the foot-long instrument of torture.

"There now," she admonished breathlessly, "let that be a lesson to all of you. I hope I never see another eraser thrown in this room!"

Making an example of a misbehavior student has been the stock in trade of teachers for hundreds of years. It seems almost intuitive that such an act should serve as a deterrent for other students who might otherwise become discipline problems. It is a way that a teacher attempts to control the rest of the class by proxy.

Is this an effective control technique? Under what conditions? With what kind of students?

Producing a Ripple Effect

Jacob Kounin (1961) and his associates observed misbehavior episodes in over 50 classrooms to determine the answers to some of these questions. They focused on four elements of every deviancy episode: the teacher, the deviant, the control technique, and the audience.

They concluded that certain characteristics of control techniques that a teacher used on a deviant produced a ripple effect which influenced the audience classmates who witnessed the episode.

Clarifying Deviancy Situations

It soon became obvious that clear control techniques produced strong, positive ripple effects. Time and again, the Kounin research team found that when teachers specified the deviancy, the deviant, and the preferred behavior, classmates of the misbehaver were less likely to get in trouble later on.

Reprimands like, "Hey you guys, cut it out!," produced little or no effect on others because they were so inexplicit that nothing about the situation was clarified.

On the other hand, when a teacher said, "Sam Hakins, you stop your whispering and fill out your workbook pages," every classmate within earshot was reminded of what constituted appropriate and inappropriate behavior. This seems to be basic to a positive ripple effect.

Miss Linders' handling of Henry's eraser throwing was quite clear. Everyone in class knew the deviant and the deviancy. But the preferred behavior, working instead of throwing, was not made explicit.

It is probable that after the first week of school the clarity of the whole classroom situation is more important to good discipline than the clarity of specific control techniques.

Being Consistently Firm

Kounin's research showed that the deviant's classmates are less likely to misbehave if the teacher's control technique is firm. Firmness can be achieved by an "I mean it!" quality in the teacher's voice, by the teacher's moving toward the culprit, and by following through after an order has been given.

The teacher who begs, "Please settle down now or I don't know what I will do," isn't creating positive ripple.

On the other hand, a teacher who "flies off the handle," "goes to pieces," and shakes or spanks a child emotionally for a minor infraction has gone beyond firmness to roughness. Rough control techniques were found to produce squirming, fidgeting and other behavior disruption inimical to learning. It is a frightening phenomenon to have the only adult in the classroom "lose his cool" and give way to intensely emotional behavior.

Miss Linders' punishment of Henry was rough. Her students probably had a hard time settling down after she whipped him.

Keeping Control Task- (Not Teacher-) Centered

Research shows that positive ripple is strengthened when the teacher uses control techniques that are based upon the demands of the learning task.

"If you don't stop daydreaming, you won't be finished in time to take the quiz," produces more positive ripple than, "Stop looking off into space, I don't allow that in my room."

Miss Linders made her control technique sound teacher-centered. She could have referred to the danger of throwing erasers or to Henry's loss of valuable learning time.

Determining the Deviant's Effect

After Kounin's group had determined the control technique characteristics that produced positive ripple, Gnagey (1960) set out to discover what characteristics of the deviant himself might be involved.

The four fifth-grade classes that were chosen for the experiment were given a pretest on their opinions about lady teachers as disciplinarians. A sociogram was also administered in order to measure the class prestige of each of the boys. Each class was also introduced to a "lady film teacher" who promised to come back and show films the next week.

Using the results of the sociogram, the male leaders and isolates were determined for each class. In two of the classes, strong male leaders were secretly trained to assist in the experiment. Two male isolates were trained to help in the other two classes.

When the day for the experiment arrived for each group, the "lady film teacher" took the class to the place where they were accustomed to watching educational movies. The teacher told them that she was interested in using films at school and wanted the class to "listen quietly, without talking" so that they could talk the film over afterward. The film teacher then turned on the projector. At a prearranged signal, the boy who was secretly trained said loudly, "Hey! Is this thing about over?" The film teacher immediately turned off the projector and said firmly, "Hey you! I told you not to talk during the film. You leave the room and go to the principal's office."

In one group, a high prestige boy had been trained to obey submissively. He lowered his eyes and said contritely, "Yes ma'am, I'm sorry ma'am." He then left the room meekly and closed the door quietly behind him.

In another class, a high prestige boy had been trained to react in a defiant manner. He said in an irritated voice, "Okay, I'll leave the room, but I won't go to the office. The heck with you!" He strode out of the room angrily and slammed the door.

The other two classes experienced exactly the same submissive or defiant responses but from the isolate boys who had virtually no influence among their peers.

After the deviants left the room, the film teacher turned the projector back on and showed the remainder of the film. At the conclusion of the film, the experimenter appeared and administered a post-test which measured the students' reactions to the incident and the amount each had learned from the film.

Measuring the Effect of the Deviant's Prestige

The results showed that large opinion changes occurred in the classes where the high prestige boys had taken the role of the deviant. Small but significant changes appeared when low prestige boys played the deviant.

Measuring the Effect of the Deviant's Response

Predictably, the class opinion seemed parallel to that expressed by the responses of the high influence deviants. In the class where the leader meekly obeyed the teacher, his classmates judged the film teacher to be a stronger disciplinarian and to know a lot about showing films. These same classmates said that her sending the deviant out was fair. They also scored high on the film test.

In the class in which the high prestige deviant angrily refused to go to the principal's office, the other students judged the lady film teacher to be a poor disciplinarian and to know little about showing films. They thought it was unfair to send a student out for talking during a film. In addition, they scored low on the film test.

These results suggested that the strength of the ripple effect is associated with the deviant's prestige, while his response to the control technique determines whether that effect will be negative or positive.

Although we have no clues about the prestige accorded to Henry Weber, Miss Linders would do well to find out who the class leaders are and to learn to discipline them effectively. This would help her control the remainder of the class by proxy.

SUMMARY

In order to produce a strong positive ripple effect on the remainder of the class, a teacher should adhere to the following principles when disciplining a misbehaving student in front of his peers.

1. Be sure your control techniques clearly specify the deviant, the deviancy and an acceptable alternative behavior.
2. Be firm about your reprimands and follow through with appropriate consequences.
3. Avoid rough, over-emotional reaction to student misbehaviors.
4. Explain your rules in terms of their effect on your students' progress rather than your own personal preferences.
5. Study your classroom leaders carefully so you are especially effective in controlling their misbehavior.

Chapter 5
Reconditioning Student Behavior

"Don't try to bring in any of that behavior modification stuff into this school system. I think it's wrong to bribe kids to learn!"

Initial responses like this one are common in some parts of the country. These same people feel that using such psychological methods smacks of brainwashing and "1984." They honestly believe that there is something underhanded and un-American about setting up a situation structured specifically to change student behavior.

But teachers have been hired for thousands of years to do just that. The more complicated a society became, the more the populace saw a need to alter the knowledge, skills and feelings of the young. Billions of dollars are spent in the U.S.A. each year in the public schools in hopes that teachers can modify the behavior of their students so they can better meet the challenges of life in a modern society.

Using Behavior Modification

Far from being either occult or scientifically sinister, behavior modification merely refers to the more systematic use of the same learning principles teachers have been using all along.

These principles can be applied to gaining academic knowledge, improving psychomotor skills, or changing student social interactions, producing what we call "good discipline."

Using Positive Reinforcement

Behavior that is rewarded usually increases in frequency. That is just another way of saying, "Nothing succeeds like success." Effective teachers have always found numerous ways to reward their students for "being smart" and "being good."

Modern psychologists have reminded teachers that it is just as important to "catch students being good" as it is to know when they are misbehaving. In fact, it is so rewarding just to be noticed by the teachers that some students will continually misbehave just to obtain the limelight for a brief moment.

Grades, happy faces, stars, honor societies and valedictories are all examples of rewards teachers have concocted to reinforce students for changing their behavior in certain directions.

Using the Extinction Principle

"Don't pay any attention to him, he's just showing off." This admonition illustrates a principle teachers have long known about. A behavior will become extinct if it doesn't pay off for a student in some way. Thus, ignoring can become a control technique in itself.

There are two major problems with ignoring. When a misbehavior is potentially dangerous to a student or his classmates, the teacher must take immediate action—even if her attention is rewarding for the culprit.

A second problem deals with rewards given by persons other than the teacher. The school clown is reinforced by his laughing classmates even though the teacher remains in stony-faced silence.

If extinction is to function as a behavior modification technique, a teacher must arrange the situation so that misbehaving brings absolutely no rewards to the deviant.

Applying Constructive Modeling

In the little red school house, a student learned how to act by watching kids in the upper grades. If the teacher was successful in keeping the older kids in line, the younger ones tended to follow their example.

In the lower grades, the teacher may wish to demonstrate the proper way to line up or sharpen a pencil. Having a class leader do the demonstration is another way of using constructive modeling.

In an earlier chapter, we described the "ripple effect." This is a special case of modeling in which the attitudes and behaviors of the audience tend to duplicate the response of a class leader to being reprimanded by the teacher.

Cueing Acceptable Behavior

Often the difference between appropriate behavior and misbehavior is a matter of timing. If the teacher can provide her students with a series of signals for various behaviors, a lot of inappropriate responses can be avoided.

A posted list of rules may act as a cue for a number of learning-appropriate behaviors.

One teacher got his students to converse in lowered tones by saying, "Now let's use our science voices."

Some teachers preview new learning experiences and tell students what cues to look for. They are then sensitized to the signals for appropriate behavior in the new situation.

The familiar piano chord is still used by many elementary teachers to cue certain class learning behaviors like moving to the story area or lining up.

Using Negative Reinforcement

If acceptable behavior gets a student "off the hook" in some way, the good behavior has been negatively reinforced.

A student sitting in an undesirable seat may be moved if he behaves himself. Similarly, in a recitation situation, a student may be afraid that his answers will appear stupid to the teacher and his classmates. His first correct answer reduces this fear and reinforces accurate recitation behavior.

A student who has been excluded from class activities may be asked to join the group again.

Using a Token Economy

In certain especially difficult classes, it is necessary to apply the principles of behavior modification in an extremely systematic way. Below is a description of one such program that was used in a class of emotionally maladjusted sixth graders.

At the beginning of each half day of school, a schedule was placed on the board so that everyone knew what subjects and activities had been planned and when they were to take place.

At the end of each half day was a recreation period reserved for playing favorite games and working on hobbies. The only way a student could take part in the recreation was to have his academic work finished and correct.

While there were some group recitation sessions, most of the subjects were studied on an individualized basis. Each student had an assignment sheet attached to his or her desk. On the sheet were detailed instructions for each subject and the number of "points" each was worth. As soon as a student had finished his arithmetic assignment, for instance, he/she would signal the teacher or one of the aides to check the work. If it was not 100 percent correct, the incorrect parts were explained and the student returned to his seat to correct them.

When the assignment was both complete and correct, the teacher made a colored check on his assignment sheet and recorded his "pay points" in a small notebook. Teachers always gave oral praise to students as they recorded their points. Later each student could draw out from this account points with which he could buy games and activities in the recreation periods.

Students who hadn't earned enough points to buy recreational activities had to stay in their seats while the rest enjoyed the fun.

With the help of the students, the games and hobbies available were constantly changed so that no one got bored with them.

A system of fines was also set up so that any student who broke an important rule could have a specified number of points taken from his account.

Since some students began earning many more points than they needed for their recreation periods, the teachers purchased a number of high cost items that could be purchased by saving up points. Afro combs, perfume, footballs, dart games, etc., were displayed along with their price until students had saved enough to purchase them.

Analyzing the Token Economy

You can readily see in the description above examples of each of the behavior modification principles we have previously discussed.

The positive reinforcements or rewards were given for completing academic work. Both points and verbal praise were used.

Not only was pay withheld for misbehavior, but deviants were often fined for breaking rules. This is called *deprivative punishment* in Chapter 6.

Although no mention was made of using modeling, misbehaving students had to watch their better behaved classmates reap the rewards of their work.

The special cueing system was provided by the schedule on the board and the individual assignment sheets.

Students who had to "sit out" the recreation periods were negatively as well as positively reinforced when their performance earned enough points to leave the sidelines and participate in the recreation periods.

SUMMARY

Behavior modification is a systematic use of learning principles to change student behavior. Every teacher must set up the classroom so that:

1. Students will be rewarded for behaving according to the rules.
2. They will get no kicks (payoff) out of misbehaving.
3. The teacher and classroom leaders demonstrate proper behavior.
4. Appropriate behaviors are signalled by a special cueing system.
5. Acceptable behavior moves students away from uncomfortable situations.

Chapter 6
Using Punishment Constructively

A tremendous amount of conflict centers around the use of punishment as a means of controlling classroom misbehavior. Opinions range all the way from those who use it almost exclusively to those who join national organizations to prohibit it altogether.

One suspects that the use of corporal punishment originated in those days when it was widely believed that misbehavior was caused by demon possession. Such phrases as "What's gotten into you?" attest to this belief.

It followed that if the devil was indeed living inside a criminal, the only way to reform him was to drive the evil spirit out. One way to do this was to inflict so much pain upon the body of the possessed that the devil would become uncomfortable and leave. We still hear some teachers say that they would like to "beat the devil out of" a particularly nasty student.

Some high schools in the 1800's published lists of student offenses and the number of lashes that must be given as punishment for each. Playing cards and swearing were punished severely (8-10 lashes), while "blotting one's copybook" was considered only a minor infraction (2 lashes).

But in this enlightened age of child psychology and learning disability clinics, some teachers still rely heavily upon harsh punishment as the main ingredient of what they call "good discipline" in the classroom. Students are still sentenced to "swats" with a wooden paddle and made to stand with heavy books in outstretched hands until they drop from exhaustion.

Avoiding Revenge

Since few people operate on the "demon possession" theory of discipline, one must conclude that an awful lot of harsh punishment is just plain revenge. Teachers would be unusual if they didn't become more than a little angry at those obstreperous students who continually thwart their carefully laid plans and disrupt their class. But revenge has a number of debilitating side effects that should be made clear.

There are two initial dangers that are associated with retributive (revenge type) punishment. The first is the possible destruction of the trust and concern relationship between the teacher and the punished student. In a relation where intercommunication is so crucial, this drawback is not to be taken lightly.

The second danger is the potentially satisfying (reinforcing) effect upon the teacher of "giving the little devils what they deserve." If harsh punishment does, in fact, act as a relaxing catharsis, a teacher may be expected to increase his punishing responses to the exclusion of many less aversive and more appropriate control techniques.

In addition, we have earlier cited four other drawbacks to the use of abrasive punishment (Gnagey, 1968).

1. Punishment tends to suppress misbehavior but does not facilitate its extinction. When a substitute teacher takes over the class of an autocrat, the poor sub often becomes the target of all the stored-up misbehavior that was regularly suppressed by punishment or the threat of it.
2. Punishment doesn't necessarily indicate the preferred alternative behaviors. If a new student is reprimanded for using the hall pass improperly, he still must be instructed in its proper use.
3. Severe punishment often causes students to avoid their academic problems rather than solve them. Since the negative emotions that accompany punishment easily become associated with elements of the surrounding environment, the teacher, the subject and the classroom may soon trigger these unfortunate feelings even when no punishment occurs. The result is often apparent in increased truancy and a higher drop-out rate.
4. Fear of punishment inhibits creativity. A student who is continually anxious about his ability to please the teacher in order to avoid punishment will seldom take the risks necessary to create new ways of solving problems. In a school system which purports to prepare future citizens who can cope with a rapidly changing society, restricting creativity could be disastrous.

In addition, punishment has often been rejected philosophically as inhumane and unprofessional (Gardner, 1969) or even cruel (Solomon, 1964).

Using Punishment Effectively

With the present popularity of behavior modification comes a focus on positive reinforcement and extinction. The teacher tries to "catch a student being good" and offer some immediate reward. If there is misbehavior, some say that it must be ignored since mere attention acts as a reinforcer for some students.

But educators realize that there are some potentially dangerous behaviors that cannot be ignored, and also that ignored behaviors may be reinforced by a student's classmates. The facts are that punishment *is* widely used and, therefore, we should know how to administer it effectively.

One recent review of the literature (MacMillan et al., 1973) cites empirical support for seven conclusions about the use of punishment. These are paraphrased below in the form of principles that teachers may use to increase the effectiveness of their punishments.

Build Positive Relationships

Punishment appears to be more effective when administered by a person with whom the student has a positive attachment (Aronfreed, 1968; Becker, 1964; Hoffman, 1963; Parke, 1970).

A number of reasons have been advanced to explain this. One contends that when a student likes a teacher, punishment is both abrasive and deprivative at the same time. When the teacher scolds (abrasive), he also appears to withhold his affection (deprivative) for the student. This withholding of affection may be anxiety arousing to the student in addition.

Punish Early and Consistently

If a student is punished as he begins to misbehave, he is less likely to repeat the deviancy than if he is punished after he completes the act. This is probably because his fear of punishment becomes associated with the initial actions or thoughts of actions and gives him time to stop before the entire deviancy is carried out.

Teachers who can see deviancies developing should stop them before they get started. Otherwise, the fear operates only after the fact.

As with rewards, punishments should be consistent—that is, rulebreakers should be punished each time they transgress. Whenever deviants get away with a misbehavior, it becomes just that much harder to get rid of.

Punishment Should Be Moderately Intense

Researchers have found that a quick, firm rebuke is much more effective than a low-keyed punishment that has to be repeated on increasingly severe levels. This does not call for inquisition techniques for every minor infraction, but it does call for reprimands that pack a wallup.

Tell Students What Behavior is Being Punished

Especially when punishment must be delayed, the teacher should verbalize the misbehavior. This brings back the incident more vividly so that the punishment is seen as a direct result of the transgression. In addition, fear becomes associated with the words so that thinking them in the future may be enough to stop the misbehavior from occurring.

Make Acceptable Alternatives Clear and Valent

Punishing a student tells him only what he did wrong. He must know what the acceptable alternatives are. Also, once he stops the unapproved behavior and makes more acceptable responses, the teacher must be ready to reward these accepted, incompatible actions. This principle reiterates a principle that we presented earlier in this chapter (see page 24).

Change Punishments Occasionally

The same punishment used over and over again, because it is so familiar and expected, loses its effectiveness. The good disciplinarian words his reprimands differently from time to time so they won't become "old hat."

SUMMARY

Because of the negative side effects, teachers should try to eliminate strongly abrasive punishment based largely on revenge. While the behavior modification approach described in Chapter 5 emphasizes the reward of acceptable behavior, there are many unacceptable behaviors that cannot be ignored until they become extinct. These may respond to the effective administration of punishment.

Applying the following principles will make punishment work better.

1. Form a warm, positive relationship with your students.
2. Punish students when they begin to misbehave rather than afterward.
3. Be consistent. Don't let students get away with punishable deviancies.
4. Use moderately intense punishment right away rather than work up to it.
5. Be sure students know exactly what behavior they are being punished for.
6. Be sure to make clear to the deviant what behaviors he should do.
7. Change your punishments occasionally. Don't always use the same ones.

Chapter 7
Increasing Self-Control

I suppose everyone agrees that student self-control is one objective of good teaching. A major objection to the use of behavior modification techniques has been the fear that once we employ rewards and punishments to control a student's misbehavior, he will require them forever after—and develop no self-control.

Many times I have heard teachers say that they made a practice of leaving their classes alone periodically so that they could learn self-control. It has never been clear to me how merely being teacherless develops self-control. In addition, unless the teacher employs spies or hidden monitoring devices, it has never been clear how they knew when and if self-control was exercised.

Defining Self-Control

What teachers usually mean by self-control is that a student behaves himself when the teacher is gone. His self-control is thought to be even greater if there is an especially tempting situation or when his or her friends are acting up.

I suppose we could formalize a definition and say, "A student exerts self-control when he obeys the classroom rules in the absence of anyone to reward or punish him."

Learning Self-Management

Mahoney and Thoresen (1972) insist that self-control is not some vague capacity called "will power," but a technology that can be learned.

They point out that behavioral self-control involves (1) the careful description of some behavior one wishes to increase or decrease, (2) the identification of the stimuli that precede it and the consequences that follow it, and (3) the changing of some of the antecedent stimuli and/or consequences.

These authors suggest that *self-observation* is the first step in learning self-control. They point to research evidence which indicates that desirable behaviors can often be increased merely by counting and recording them. One teacher who was conducting an experiment in behavior modification found that the out-of-seat behavior that she was recording for a baseline stopped completely when her students guessed what she was tallying. In a way, self-observation may increase the clarity referred to in Chapter 4.

Environmental planning is the second step in Mahoney and Thoresen's approach. This involves making changes in one's own surroundings by altering the stimuli which seem to trigger a behavior and the rewards or punishments which follow it. Redl and Wineman (1957) make use of this step when they suggest "temptation removal" as an effective control technique. This is another illustration of the "cueing principle" which we referred to in the "reconditioning chapter."

Behavioral programming is the third self-control strategy suggested by the authors. This entails self-reward and self-punishment. Rewards can vary from giving oneself a verbal pat on the back to taking an extra helping of dessert. Some students condition themselves to study by rewarding themselves with a "Coke break" after each assignment has been finished.

Likewise, self-punishment may vary from imagining oneself distorted and obese after overeating to actually slapping one's own wrists. One psychologist conditioned his obese subjects to stay on their diets by having them break something they valued if they didn't make their weight loss goal.

Several recent studies have shown that students can change their own behaviors by using the three strategies described above (Bolstad and Johnson, 1972; Gottman and McFall, 1972; Knapczyk and Livingston, 1973).

Teaching Self-Control

Two kinds of benefits could accrue from teaching students the three self-control strategies described above. The obvious one is that learning-appropriate behaviors would increase and disciplinary problems would decrease.

Perhaps a more important outcome would be the increase in student self-mastery. As pupils learn how to change themselves, they are freer to direct their own actions and more able to function in a civilized manner without external coercion.

To summarize, Mahoney and Thoresen describe self-control as a person's use of behavior modification principles to change his own actions. The following steps may be taken to implement these procedures in the classroom.

1. Describe the misbehavior clearly so the student knows exactly what he has been doing. Be sure he has just as clear a picture of what he should do instead.
2. Ask the student to count the times he breaks the rule and note what happens just before and right after he misbehaves.
3. Help the student change the stimuli which come just before the misbehavior or punish himself immediately after he misbehaves.
4. Ask the student to count and record the times he does the preferred action and reward himself immediately afterward.
5. By explaining the principles and using many illustrations, help students learn this general sequence for other situations calling for self-control.

Punishment and Self-Control

Justin Aronfreed has written extensively about the relationship between punishment and self-control (1960, 1961, 1963, 1965). Unlike the Mahoney-Thoresen approach, Aronfreed experiments with what can be done *to* children that will keep them from misbehaving when the teacher is absent.

This author insists that self-control results from punishment. He points out that when punishment follows any behavior, fear becomes associated with the behavior itself and with inner thoughts of the behavior.

The fear then motivates a student to avoid the misbehavior so that he will not be punished.

Aronfreed's experiments suggest that if students are to behave themselves in the absence of a punisher, the timing of the punishment is important. If a student gets social punishment as he begins the misbehavior instead of after he has completed it, he is more likely to take the blame for the misdeeds and make proper restitution.

This author also found that restitution is more likely when students have had a part in setting the punishment and when evaluative labels (bad, horrid, naughty, etc.) are attached to the punishment.

SUMMARY

The classroom teacher who wishes students to behave during times when he is out of the room should follow these general principles.

1. Monitor pupils' behaviors closely so that you can catch them as they begin to break a rule.
2. Always give verbal punishment along with any other you may use. Put in evaluative words such as naughty, bad, horrid, uncouth, etc.
3. Confer with students about what punishments they think are fair.

Chapter 8
Applying Glasser's Reality Therapy: An Eclectic Approach

"Dan, what did I just see you doing?" said Miss White pointedly.

"I was just resting my eyes," blurted the surprised lad.

"What else were you doing?" persisted the teacher, moving closer to Dan and lowering her voice to avoid distracting the others.

"What do you mean?" hedged Dan, "I am just taking the test like everyone else."

"I mean I saw you doing something else and I want to know what it was," Miss White continued doggedly.

By this time, Dan's face had reddened and the beginnings of tears were in his eyes. "I was cheating," he blurted. "I copied some answers from Gretchen's paper—I'm sorry."

"But Gretchen has a different form of the test," said the teacher, "all the answers you copied will be wrong!"

Dan shook his head miserably as he blew his nose and fought back the tears. It was bad enough getting caught copying but to find out that he had been tricked was even worse. Dan braced for the tirade he knew he deserved.

"Well," queried Miss White frankly, "did cheating help you get a good grade?"

"No," rejoined Dan resignedly, "It only got me in trouble again. My dad will kill me!"

"What plans do you have that will keep it from happening again," asked the teacher evenly. "You know we've got to do something about it!"

"How about making me sit in the back by the sink so I can't see anybody's paper," offered Dan, still half expecting to be punished for his offense.

"Okay," said Miss White amicably. "You can move back there for the rest of this period. Next time, you can sit back there for the entire test."

The incident above illustrates in a simplified fashion the way a teacher can use William Glasser's Reality Therapy in dealing with classroom misbehavior.

Since it is an eclectic approach to discipline, we will use it as a vehicle for tying together many of the principles that have been presented in the earlier chapters.

Five Basic Elements of Discipline

Glasser believes that discipline involves a student's understanding the need to obey reasonable rules and regulations so that everyone can have a better life. Punishment, on the other hand, concerns the enforcement of the rules with the threat of pain.

In order to produce good discipline in a school, Glasser believes that five basic elements must obtain:

1. *School must be a good place.* If the students like the school and find school people thoughtful, friendly and bent on helping them succeed, then good discipline is enhanced. We have previously pointed out (Chapter 6) that even punishment is more effective when it is administered by teachers who are liked by their misbehaving students. We have also alluded to the importance of academic assistance as a means of eliminating frustration-based aggression (Chapter 3). If school is a good place, positive reinforcement (Chapter 5) should be plentiful.

2. *Students must know the school rules.* If a teacher's behavioral expectations are clear to his students, there is a lot better chance for those preferred behaviors to increase. We have already discussed the benefits of "clarity" in connection with the production of a positive ripple effect (Chapter 4). We also pointed out that punishment is more effective when the deviants know what they are being punished for (Chapter 6).

3. *Within reason, students should agree with the rules.* Glasser insists that if the rules make sense and promise to produce a better learning situation for all, students will welcome them. You will remember that positive ripple resulted from "task-centered" control techniques which emphasize cause and effect on the student's assignment (Chapter 4).

4. *Students should participate in rule-making.* Since classroom situations are always changing, rules should be changeable also. When students have a part in making and changing rules, better discipline usually results. Although this would certainly increase clarity, Glasser's system is the only one in this book that emphasizes student participation in rule-making. The point was made in Chapter 6 that punishment is more effective when students have a part in its planning.

5. *Students should know the consequences of rule breaking.* If a student contemplates breaking the rules, he should know the price he will have to pay. If the price is logically related to the misbehavior, better discipline will result. This is not only congruent with the "task-centered" aspect of good control techniques (Chapter 4) but suggests the consistency referred to in the punishment chapter (Chapter 6).

Steps in Reality Therapy

Securing Student Involvement. In order for reality therapy to work, teachers and students must be involved in warm, personal relationships with each other. This includes honest, interested interactions which inspire trust and concern. This is part of making school a good place and is related to all the principles reviewed there.

Identifying Problem Behavior. Before helping a student change his irresponsible behavior, the teacher must make him aware of the misbehavior he is doing now. In the opening example, Miss White kept questioning Dan until he admitted the copying offense.

But notice also that the teacher didn't demand to know why. This would only invite Dan to make up excuses instead of taking responsibility for his actions. Notice also that Miss White didn't bring up all Dan's past "sins" either. The principal intent was to get Dan to identify his own misbehavior as a starting point.

In the "self-control" chapter (7), "self-observation" was also cited as a beginning point for changing one's own behavior. It is probable that both of these are strongly related to clarity.

Evaluating Inappropriate Behavior. When Miss White asked Dan, "Well, did cheating help you get a good grade?" she was asking him to judge his own behavior critically in terms of its effectiveness in reaching his goals.

Since Dan knew that his teacher cared about him and respected him, he was able to make the judgment that his answer copying was not helpful. This is especially important in reality therapy since it is based on the assumption that the student alone is responsible for his own behavior.

The emphasis on cause and effect here is certainly related to the "task-centeredness" of effective control techniques. It is also connected to anticipated reinforcement and, therefore, squares with Chapter 5.

Planning New Behavior. Having identified and evaluated his misbehavior, a student must be encouraged to set up a plan of action to solve the problem. Since the irresponsible student may not have had much experience developing such plans, the teacher should encourage him not to attempt too much at once. Dan's suggestion to move his seat was probably better than attempting a complete revision of his study habits so he would not need to cheat.

In addition, the teacher must make it clear that all plans are tentative. If the first plan doesn't work, another one should be developed. This doesn't mean that a student should be allowed to abdicate his responsibility to carry out a feasible plan.

If a student's plan has elements that are clearly unacceptable to the teacher, he must say so and ask the student to come up with another alternative.

The emphasis on a deviant's planning his new behavior certainly underscores "behavioral programming" referred to in the "self-control" chapter.

Gaining Commitment. Miss White must get Dan to make an oral or written commitment to his plan. Unless he agrees to put the plan into operation and unless someone else knows about the promise, it may be easier to let things slide.

With the exception of the probability that self-planning may increase personal involvement, Glasser's insistence upon a more or less "public" commitment to a plan of action is unique among the systems described in this book.

Accepting No Excuses. A misbehaving student often fails to fulfill his initial commitment. When this happens, the teacher should help him back up a step and reevaluate his inappropriate behavior. If he still is convinced that it was ineffective, he must recommit himself to the plan and be ready to take the consequences of his behavior. The teacher should never accept excuses—only recommitments or alternative plans.

This is certainly an aspect of both consistency and follow-through. The focus on consequences dovetails nicely with the "reconditioning" chapter.

Avoiding Punishment. Beatings, threats and ridicule only break down the involvement relationship between the teacher and the irresponsible student. The teacher must stand by the plan and the consequences, but the latter should be a logical result of the misbehavior.

Glasser reiterates at least one of the drawbacks listed for abrasive punishment. His insistence on logical results suggests task-centeredness once more.

Classroom Meetings

Glasser (1969) suggests the use of classroom meetings to solve social problems. In this way, the whole class becomes involved in solving individual and group problems.

Acting as a group leader, the teacher encourages all members of the class to participate and uses the following guidelines:

1. The class members should sit in a circle.
2. Any individual or group problems may be brought up by individual students and discussed by the group.
3. The discussion should avoid punishment or fault-finding and should center on finding more effective ways for students to behave.

SUMMARY

Glasser believes that students will obey reasonable rules and regulations when they understand how these rules can produce a better life for everyone. The following basic elements will help bring this about:

1. School must be a good place.
2. Students must know the rules.
3. Students should agree with the rules.
4. Students should help make the rules.
5. Students should know what will happen if they break the rules.

When students do misbehave, the following steps should help correct the situation:

1. Secure student involvement.
2. Help the student identify the problem behavior.
3. Help the student evaluate the effects of his misbehavior.
4. Assist the student in planning new acceptable behavior.
5. Gain the students' commitment to the plan.
6. Accept no excuses for failure to follow the plan.
7. Avoid punishing deviant students.

Discipline may be improved by holding informal classroom discussions that focus on finding more effective ways for students to behave.

Appendix A
Check List for Evaluating Your Disciplinary Techniques

The check list below is a summary of the disciplinary principles described in Chapters 2-8 in this book. A check on the proper line will help you discover your effective and ineffective procedures. All items that are rated "sometimes" or "seldom" call for active improvement on your part.

CHECK LIST

Usually / Sometimes / Seldom

Preventing Classroom Misbehavior

___ ___ ___ Are your transitions smooth?
___ ___ ___ Are your lessons free from slowdowns?
___ ___ ___ Do you keep your students alert and accountable?
___ ___ ___ Do your lessons contain sufficient variety?
___ ___ ___ Do you handle overlapping situations well?
___ ___ ___ Are you alert to what you students are doing in class?

Controlling Deviants Directly

___ ___ ___ Do you help students master difficult skills and concepts?
___ ___ ___ Do you switch to new teaching approaches when the old ones don't work?
___ ___ ___ Do you remove distractions from your classroom?
___ ___ ___ Do you help students develop effective routines for taking care of their daily chores?

Usually	Sometimes	Seldom	
___	___	___	Do you practice emergency procedures (fire, disaster, etc.) sufficiently?
___	___	___	Are you able to help students laugh off their tensions when appropriate?
___	___	___	Do you use unobtrusive visual signals to cue usually well-behaved students?
___	___	___	Do you ask "off the track" students questions that remind them of their goals?
___	___	___	Do you help misbehaving students understand the probable results of their actions?

Controlling Deviants by Proxy

___	___	___	Are your control techniques clear?
___	___	___	Are your control techniques firm but not rough?
___	___	___	Are your control techniques task-centered rather than teacher-centered?
___	___	___	Are you successful in controlling your class leaders?

Reconditioning Student Behavior

___	___	___	Do you reward students for behaving appropriately?
___	___	___	Are you able to ignore harmless deviancies?
___	___	___	Do you demonstrate the preferred classroom behaviors yourself?
___	___	___	Do you use effective cues for eliciting approved behavior?
___	___	___	Do you make use of negative reinforcement for acceptable behavior?

Using Punishment Constructively

___	___	___	Are you able to avoid taking revenge on a misbehaving student?
___	___	___	Do you use deprivative punishment?
___	___	___	Do you work at building positive relationships with your students?
___	___	___	Do you punish your students as their deviancies begin to emerge rather than after the misbehavior is over?
___	___	___	Do you punish students consistently for breaking the rules?
___	___	___	Are you careful to let students know the behavior they are being punished for?
___	___	___	Do you change your punishments periodically?

Increasing Self-Control

___	___	___	Do you describe a deviant's misbehavior clearly so he knows what he has done wrong?
___	___	___	Do you encourage pupil self-observation?
___	___	___	Do you help misbehaving students change the environment that triggers their deviancies?

CHECK LIST FOR EVALUATING YOUR DISCIPLINARY TECHNIQUES

Usually	Sometimes	Seldom	
___	___	___	Do you help your deviant students reward and punish themselves to improve their school-appropriate behavior?
___	___	___	Do you help students know and understand the principles of developing self-control?
___	___	___	Do you give verbal punishment whenever you use other forms?
___	___	___	Do you confer with your students about what punishments they believe are fair?

Applying Glasser's Reality Therapy

___	___	___	Is your classroom a pleasant place for students to be?
___	___	___	Do your students know what the rules are?
___	___	___	Do your students agree with your rules?
___	___	___	Do you allow your students to participate in making the rules of the classroom?
___	___	___	Do your students know what the consequences are for breaking classroom rules?
___	___	___	Do you follow Glasser's seven steps in reality therapy?
___	___	___	Do you use classroom meetings to solve disciplinary problems?

Appendix B
References

Adams, Gerald R. "Classroom Aggression: Determinants, Controlling Mechanisms, and Guidelines for the Implementation of a Behavior Modification Program," *Psychology in the Schools,* 10 (1973), 155–168.

Aronfreed, J. "Aversive Control of Socialization," in W. J. Arnold (ed.), *Nebraska Symposium on Motivation 1968*. Lincoln: University of Nebraska Press, 1968.

——— "Moral Behavior and Sex Identity," in D. R. Miller and G. E. Swanson (eds.), *Inner Conflict and Defense.* New York: Holt, Rinehart and Winston, 1960.

——— "Punishment Learning and Internalization: Some Parameters of Reinforcement and Cognition." Paper presented at the Biennial Meeting of the Society for Research in Child Development, Minneapolis, Minnesota, March, 1965.

——— "The Effect of Experimental Socialization Paradigms Upon Two Moral Responses to Transgression," *Journal of Abnormal Social Psychology,* 66 (1963), 437–448.

——— "The Nature, Variety and Social Patterning of Moral Responses to Transgression," *Journal of Abnormal and Social Psychology,* 63 (1961), 223–240.

——— "The Origins of Self-Criticism," *Psychological Review,* 71 (1964), 193–218.

Aronfreed, J., R. A. Cutlick, and S. A. Fagan. "Cognitive Structure, Punishment and Nurturance in the Experimental Inductions of Self-Criticism," *Child Development,* 34 (1963), 281–294.

Aronfreed, J., and A. Reber. "Internalized Behavioral Suppression and The Timing of Social Punishment," *Journal of Personality and Social Psychology,* 1 (1965), 3-16.

Aronson, E., and J. M. Carlsmith. "Effect of the Severity of Threat on The Devaluation of Forbidden Behavior," *Journal of Abnormal and Social Psychology,* 66 (1963), 504-588.

Bandura, A. "Punishment Revisited," *Journal of Consulting Psychology,* 26 (1962), 298-301.

Bandura, A., and T. L. Rosenthal. "Vicarious Classical Conditioning As A Function of Arousal Level," *Journal of Personality and Social Psychology,* 3 (1966), 54-62.

Bandura, R., D. Ross, and S. A. Ross. "Vicarious Reinforcement and Imitative Learning," *Journal of Abnormal and Social Psychology,* 67 (1963), 601-607.

Barrish, H. H., M. Saunders, and M. M. Wolf. "Good Behavior Game: Effects of Individual Contingencies for Group Consequences on Disruptive Behavior in a Classroom," *Journal of Applied Behavior Analysis,* 2 (1969), 119-124.

Becker, Wesley C. "Applications of Behavior Principles in Typical Classrooms," in C. E. Thoresen (ed.), *Behavior Modification in Education: I.* Chicago: National Society for the Study of Education, 1972.

Becker, W. C. "Consequences of Different Kinds of Parental Discipline," in M. L. Hoffman and L. W. Hoffman (eds.), *Review of Child Development Research,* Vol. 1. New York: Russell Sage Foundation, 1964.

Becker, W. C., C. H. Madsen, C. R. Arnold, and D. Thomas. "Contingent Use of Teacher Attention and Praise in Reducing Classroom Behavior Problems," *Journal of Special Education,* 1 (1967), 287-307.

Biaggio, Angela, and Aroldo Rodriques. "Behavioral Compliance and Devaluation of the Forbidden Object as a Function of Probability of Detection and Severity of Threat," *Developmental Psychology,* 4 (1971), 320-323.

Bolstad, Orin D., and Stephen M. Johnson. "Self-Regulation in the Modification of Disruptive Classroom Behavior," *Journal of Applied Behavior Analysis,* 5 (1972), 443-454.

Booth, James, and G. Wayne Shamo. "Punishment--A Condition of Learning," *College Student Journal,* 6 (1972), 74-77.

Brody, Charles, Robert Plutchik, Edwina Reilly, and Martin Peterson. "Personality and Problem Behavior of Third-Grade Children in Regular Classes," *Psychology in the Schools,* 10 (1973), 196-199.

Bushell, D., P. A. Wrobel, and M. L. Michaelis. "Applying 'Group' Contingencies to the Classroom Study Behavior of Preschool Children," *Journal of Applied Behavior Analysis,* 1 (1968), 55-61.

Cangemi, Joseph P., and Kanwar H. Khan. "The Psychology of Punishment and the Potential School Dropout." *Education,* 94 (1973), 117-119.

Cellar, S. "Practices Associated with Effective Discipline," *Journal of Experimental Education,* 19 (1951), 333-358.

Clark, Hewitt B., Trudylee Rowbury, Ann M. Baer, and Donald M. Baer. "Timeout As a Punishing Stimulus in Continuous and Intermittent Schedules," *Journal of Applied Behavior Analysis*, 6 (1973), 443-455.

Clarizio, H. F., and S. L. Yelon. "Learning Theory Approaches to Classroom Management: Rationale and Intervention Techniques," *Journal of Special Education*, 1 (1967), 267-274.

Cobb, Joseph A. "Relationship of Discrete Classroom Behaviors to Fourth-Grade Academic Achievement," *Journal of Educational Psychology*, 63 (1972), 74-80.

Csapo, Marg. "Peer Models Reverse the One Bad Apple Spoils the Barrel Theory," *Teaching Exceptional Children*, 5 (1972), 20-24.

Cummins, Emery J. "Are Disciplinary Students Different?", *Personnel and Guidance Journal*, February (1966), 624-627.

Dietz, Samuel M., and Alan C. Repp. "Decreasing Classroom Misbehavior Through The Use of DRL Schedules of Reinforcement," *Journal of Applied Behavior Analysis*, 6 (1973), 457-463.

"Discipline--The Most Perplexing Subject of All." Panel discussion with John Holt, Haim Ginott, Lee Salk, and Donald Barr, *Teacher*, 90 (1972), 54-56.

Dixon, Carol. "Guided Options as a Pattern of Control in a Headstart Program," *Urban Life and Culture*, 1 (1972), 203-216.

Dobson, Russell, and Mary Dobson. "Elementary Students' Behavioral Problems: Teacher Perception and Treatment," *Journal of the Student Personnel Association for Teacher Education*, 7 (1968-1969), 33-42.

Dobson, Russell, Ron Goldenberg, and Bill Elsom. "Pupil Control Ideology and Teacher Influence in the Classroom," *Journal of Educational Research*, 66 (1972), 76-80.

Dobson, Russell, and others. "Teachers' and Students' Perceptions of Behavioral Problems and Prescribed Treatments," *Journal of the Student Personnel Association for Teacher Education*, 9 (1971), 97-105.

Drabman, Ronald and Robert Spitalnik. "Social Isolation as a Punishment Procedure: A Controlled Study," *Journal of Experimental Child Psychology*, 16 (1973), 236-249.

Eleftherios, Christos P., John T. Shoudt, and Harold R. Strang. "The Game Machine: A Technological Approach to Classroom Control," *Journal of School Psychology*, 10 (1972), 55-60.

Evans, G., and G. Azwalt. "Acceleration of Academic Progress Through the Manipulation of Peer Influence," *Behavior Research and Therapy*, 5 (1967), 1-7.

Feldhusen, J. F., J. R. Thurston, and J. J. Benning, "Classroom Behavior, Intelligence and Achievement," *The Journal of Experimental Education*, 36 (1967), 82-87.

Feldhusen, John F., John R. Thurston, and James J. Benning, "Aggressive Classroom Behavior and School Achievement," *Journal of Special Education*, 4 (1970), 431-439.

Fisher, R. E. "Classroom Behavior and The Body Image Boundary." *Journal of Projective Techniques and Personality Assessment*, 32 (1968), 450-452.

Forness, Steven R. "Behavioristic Approach to Classroom Management and Motivation," *Psychology in the Schools*, 7 (1970), 356-363.

Gamsky, Neal R., and Faye W. Lloyd. "Relationship of Classroom Behavior to Visual Perceptual Deficiencies," *Psychology in the Schools*, 8 (1971), 60-61.

Gardner, W. I. "Use of Punishment with the Severely Retarded: A Review," *American Journal of Mental Deficiency*, 74 (1969), 86-103.

Glasser, William, *Schools Without Failure*. New York: Harper and Row, 1969.

Gnagey, William J. "Classroom Discipline," in D. W. Allen and E. Seifman, *Teacher's Handbook*. Glenview, Illinois: Scott, Foresman and Company, 1971.

────── "Classroom Discipline," in *Encyclopedia of Education*. New York: Macmillan, 1971.

────── "Controlling Classroom Misbehavior," *NJEA Review*, 46 (1973), 24-25, 61.

────── "Deviancy: When Behavior is Misbehavior," in W. C. Morse and G. M. Wingo, *Classroom Psychology*; *Readings in Educational Psychology*. Glenview, Illinois: Scott, Foresman and Company, 1971.

────── "Do Our Schools Prevent or Promote Delinquency?," *Journal of Educational Research*, 50 (1956), 215-219.

────── "Effects on Classmates of a Deviant Student's Power and Response to a Teacher-Exerted Control Technique," *Journal of Educational Psychology*, 51 (1960), 1-9.

────── "Good Classroom Discipline Can Be Taught," in Noll and Noll, *Readings in Educational Psychology*. New York: Macmillan, 1968.

────── *Improving Classroom Discipline* (set of instructional tapes). Chicago, Illinois: Instructional Dynamics Incorporated, 1971.

────── "Social Power Structure in a Class as a Factor in the Effect of a Discipline Measure," in Raymond Kuhlen, *Studies in Educational Psychology*. Lexington, Md.: Blaisdell Publishing Company, 1967.

────── "Student Attitude Learning as a Function of Parental Acceptance and Sex of Teacher," *Journal of Teacher Education*, 19 (1968), 313-316.

────── *The Psychology of Discipline in the Classroom*. New York: Macmillan, 1968.

────── *What Research Says to the Teacher About Controlling Classroom Misbehavior*. Washington, D. C.: National Education Association, 1965.

Gottman, John M., and Richard M. McFall. "Self-Monitoring Effects in a Program for Potential High School Dropouts: A Time-Series Analysis," *Journal of Consulting and Clinical Psychology*, 39 (1972), 273-281.

Grandy, Gordon S., Charles H. Madsen, and Lois M. De Mersseman. "The Effects of Individual and Interdependent Contingencies of Inappropriate Classroom Behavior," *Psychology in the Schools*, 10 (1973), 488-493.

Greene, J. E. "Alleged Misbehaviors Among High School Students," *Journal of Social Psychology*, 58 (1962), 371–382.

Gump, P. V., and J. S. Kounin. "Issues Raised by Ecological and 'Classical' Research Efforts," *Merrill-Palmer Quarterly of Behavior and Development*, 6 (1959–1960), 145–152.

Hagebak, Robert W. "Disciplinary Practices in Dallas Contrasted with School Systems with Rules Against Violence Against Children," *Journal of Clinical Child Psychology*, 2 (1973), 14–16.

Hall, R. V., M. Panyan, D. Rabar, and M. Broden. "Instructing Beginning Teachers in Reinforcement Procedures Which Improve Classroom Control," *Journal of Applied Behavior Analysis*, 1 (1968), 315–322.

Hamblin, R. L., D. Buckholdt, D. Bushell, E. Desmond, and D. Ferritor. "Changing the Game from 'Get the Teacher' to 'Learn'," *Trans-Action*, 6 (1969), 20–31.

Happel, Lester C. "Patterns of Interference in an Elementary School," *Psychology in the Schools*, 9 (1972), 134–143.

Harris, V. William and James A. Sherman. "Use and Analysis of the 'Good Behavior Game' to Reduce Disruptive Classroom Behavior," *Journal of Applied Behavior Analysis*, 6 (1973), 405–417.

Hermine, H. Marshall. "The Effect of Punishment on Children: A Review of the Literature and a Suggested Hypothesis," *The Journal of Genetic Psychology*, 106 (1965), 23–33.

Hillman, Bill W. "The Family Constellation: A Clue to the Behavior of Elementary School Children," *Elementary School Guidance and Counseling*, 7 (1972), 20–25.

Hoffman, M. L. "Childbearing Practices and Moral Development: Generalization From Empirical Research," *Child Development*, 34 (1963), 295–318.

Homme, Lloyd. *How to Use Contingency Contracting in the Classroom*. Champaign, Illinois: Research Press, 1969.

Homme, L. E., P. C. deBaca, J. V. Devine, R. Steinhorst, and E. J. Rickert. "Use of the Premack Principle in Controlling the Behavior of Nursery School Children," *Journal of the Experimental Analysis of Behavior*, 6 (1963), 544.

Jenison, Lynn M. "Attitudes of Students and Faculty Toward Selected Disciplinary Situations," *NASPA Journal*, 9 (1972), 291–294.

Jones, Paul, and Jacob W. Blankenship. "The Relationship of Pupil Control Ideology and Innovative Classroom Practices," *Journal of Research in Science Teaching*, 9 (1972), 281–285.

Kagan, Jerome. "The Concept of Identification," *Psychological Review*, 65 (1958), 296–305.

Kaplan, Bert L. "Classroom Discipline Is More Than Technique," *Elementary School Journal*, 72 (1973), 244–250.

Katz, Roger C. "Interactions Between The Facilitative and Inhibitory Effects of a Punishing Stimulus in the Control of Children's Hitting Behavior," *Child Development*, 42 (1971), 1433–1446.

Kauffman, James M., and Daniel P. Hallahan. "Control of Rough Physical Behavior Using Novel Contingencies and Directive Teaching," *Perceptual and Motor Skills*, 36 (1973), 1225-1226.

Kelman, H. C. "Compliance, Identification and Internalization: Three Processes of Attitude Change," *Journal of Conflict Resolution*, 2 (1958), 51-60.

Kerrsey, David W. "Systematic Exclusion: Eliminating Chronic Classroom Disruptions," in Krumboltz and Thoresen (eds.), *Behavioral Counseling: Cases and Techniques*. New York: Holt, Rinehart and Winston, 1969.

Knafle, June B. "The Relationship of Behavior Ratings to Grades Earned by Female High School Students," *Journal of Educational Research*, 66 (1972), 106-110.

Knapczyk, Dennis R., and Gary Livingston. "Self-Recording and Student Teacher Supervision: Variables Within a Token Economy Structure," *Journal of Applied Behavior Analysis*, 6 (1973), 481-486.

Kohlberg, L. "Moral Development and Identification," *Child Psychology*, 9 (1963), 277-332.

Kounin, Jacob S. "An Analysis of Teachers' Managerial Techniques," *Psychology in the Schools*, 4 (1967), 221-227.

──── *Discipline and Group Management in Classrooms*. New York: Holt, Rinehart and Winston, 1970.

──── "Observations and Analysis of Classroom Management." Paper read at AERA, Wayne State University, 1967.

Kounin, Jacob S., and P. V. Gump. "The Comparative Influence of Punitive and Non-punitive Teachers upon Children's Concepts of School Misconduct," *Journal of Educational Psychology*, 52 (1967), 44-49.

Kounin, J. S., and P. V. Gump. "The Ripple Effect on Discipline," *Elementary School Journal*, 59 (1958), 158-162.

Kounin, J. S., P. V. Gump., and J. Ryan. "Explorations in Classroom Management," *Journal of Teacher Education*, 12 (1961), 235-246.

Kounin, J. S., and S. Obradovic. "Managing Emotionally Disturbed Children in Regular Classrooms: A Replication and Extension," *The Journal of Special Education*, 2 (1968), 129-135.

Krelis, Richard L. "Teacher Perceptions of Children's Moral Behavior," *Psychology in the Schools*, 6 (1969), 394-395.

Kuypers, D. S., W. C. Becker, and K. D. O'Leary. "How to Make a Token System Fail," *Exceptional Children*, 35 (1968), 101, 109.

Kvareceus, W. C. *Juvenile Delinquency and the School*. New York: World Book Company, 1945.

LaBelle, Thomas J., and Val D. Rust. "Control Mechanics and Their Justifications in Preschool Classrooms," *Small Group Behavior*, 4 (1973), 35-46.

Leppert, Edward, and Wayne K. Hoy. "Teacher Personality and Pupil Control Ideology," *Journal of Experimental Education*, 40 (1972), 57-59.

Long, James D., and Robert L. Williams. "The Comparative Effectiveness of Group and Individually Contingent Free Time with Inner-city Junior High School Students," *Journal of Applied Behavior Analysis*, 6 (1973), 465-474.

Lorber, N. M. "Inadequate Social Acceptance and Disruptive Classroom Behavior," *Journal of Educational Research,* 59 (1966), 360–362.

Lovitt, Thomas C., Althea O. Lovitt, Marie D. Eaton, and Mary Kirkwood. "The Deceleration of Inappropriate Comments by a Natural Consequence," *Journal of School Psychology*, 11 (1973), 148–154.

MacMillan, Donald L., Steven R. Forness, and Barbara M. Trumbull. "The Role of Punishment in The Classroom," *Exceptional Children*, 40 (1973), 85–96.

Madsen, C. H., W. C. Becker, and D. R. Thomas. "Rules, Praise and Ignoring: Elements of Elementary Classroom Control," *Journal of Applied Behavior Analysis,* 1 (1968), 139–150.

Madsen, Charles H., and Clifford K. Madsen, *Teaching/Discipline.* Boston: Allyn and Bacon, Inc., 1970.

Madsen, Charles H., Jr. and others. "Classroom RAID (Rules, Approval, Ignore, Disapproval)—A Cooperative Approach for Professionals and Volunteers, *Journal of School Psychology*, 8 (1970), 180–184.

Mahoney, Michael J., and Carl E. Thoresen. "Behavioral Self-Control—Power to the Person," *Educational Researcher,* 1 (1972), 5–7.

Medland, Michael B., and Thomas J. Stachnik. "Good-behavior Game: A Replication and Systematic Analysis," *Journal of Applied Behavior Analysis*, 5 (1972), 45–51.

Mehrens, W. A., and R. Esposito. "Teachers Perceptions of the Seriousness of Behavior Problems," *Journal of Human Relations*, 16 (1968), 97–112.

Mercurio, Joseph A. "Corporal Punishment in the School: The Plight of the First Year Teacher," *New Zealand Journal of Educational Studies,* 7 (1972), 144–152.

Nelson, Carol A. "An Analysis of Fear: Discipline," *Psychology*, 6 (1969), 15–18.

Nighswander, J. K., and G. R. Mayer. "Catharsis: A Means of Reducing Elementary School Students' Aggressive Behaviors?", *Personnel and Guidance Journal,* 47 (1969), 461–466.

O'Leary, K. D., and W. C. Becker. "Behavior Modification of an Adjustment Class: A Token Reinforcement Program," *Exceptional Children*, 33 (1967), 637–642.

O'Leary, K. D., and W. C. Becker. "The Effects of the Intensity of a Teacher's Reprimands on Children's Behavior," *Journal of School Psychology,* 7 (1968–1969), 8–11.

Parke, R. D. "The Role of Punishment in the Socialization Process," in R. A. Hoppe, G. A. Milton and E. Simmel (eds.), *Early Experiences in the Processes of Socialization.* New York: Academic Press, 1970.

Parker, James L. "Introversion/Extroversion and Children's Aversion to Social Isolation and Corporal Punishment: A Note on a Failure to Replicate Eysenck," *Australian Journal of Psychology,* 24 (1972), 141–143.

Redl, Fritz. "Before You Go Back to Your Classroom—Remember This," in *When We Deal With Children*. New York: The Free Press, 1966.

Redl, F., and D. Wineman. *The Aggressive Child*. New York: Free Press, 1957.

Redl, F., and W. Wattenberg. "Influence Techniques," in *Mental Hygiene in Teaching*. New York: Harcourt Brace Jovanovich, 1959.

Rhodes, W. "The Disturbing Child: A Problem of Ecological Management," in Graubard (ed.), *Children Against Schools*. Chicago: Follett Educational Corporation, 1969.

Rosen, Dennis C., and Terrence J. Piper. "Individualized Instruction With and Without a Token Economy in a Class for Disruptors," *Education and Training of the Mentally Retarded*, 7 (1972). 22-25.

Rowe, Wayne, Gary Williams, and Russel Harmelink. "An Alternating Program for Problem Students Based on Behavioral Precepts: Description and Preliminary Report," *Michigan Personnel and Guidance Journal*, 3 (1972), 14-19.

Rudner, Howard L. "A Practical Model for Controlling a Group of Behaviour Problems in the Classroom," *Canadian Counsellor*, 7 (1973), 119-125.

Schiller, Clarke E., George J. Michel, and Donn L. Wadley. "Sound and Student Behavior," *Audiovisual Instruction*, 14 (1969), 92.

Schmidt, G. W., and R. E. Ulrich. "Effects of Group Contingent Events Upon Classroom Noise," *Journal of Behavioral Analysis*, 2 (1969), 171.

Schwebel, Andrew I., and Dennis L. Cherlin. "Physical and Social Distancing in Teacher-Pupil Relationships," *Journal of Educational Psychology*, 63 (1972), 543-550.

Sheppard, Chris. "The Use of a Response-Cost Punishment Technique to Decrease the Disruptive Classroom Behaviors of a Group of 7th and 8th Graders," *SALT: School Application of Learning Theory*, 4 (1971), 22-26.

Sklar, Mark J., and Joanne Rampulla. "Decreasing Inappropriate Classroom Behavior of a Multiply Handicapped Blind Student," *Education of the Visually Handicapped*, 5 (1973), 71-74.

Smith, Lucille W., and Philip G. Kapfer. "Classroom Management of Learning Package Programs," *Educational Technology*, 12 (1972), 80-85.

Solomon, R. L. "Punishment," *American Psychologist*, 19 (1964), 239-253.

Spencer, Richard J. "An Empirical Study of Elementary Teacher's Attention As Reinforcement for Student Behavior," *Child Study Journal*, 3 (1973), 145-158.

Spivack, George, and Marshall S. Swift. "Achievement Related Classroom Behavior of Secondary School Normal and Disturbed Students," *Exceptional Children*, 35 (1969), 677-684.

Spivack, George, and Marshall S. Swift. "Clarifying the Relationship Between Academic Success and Overt Classroom Behavior," *Exceptional Children*, 36 (1969), 99-104.

Spivack, George, Marshall Swift, and Judith Prewitt. "Syndromes of Disturbed Classroom Behavior: A Behavioral Diagnostic System for Elementary Schools," *Journal of Special Education*, 5 (1971), 269-292.

Srivastava, Gyananand P. "Personality Traits Differences Among Disciplined and Undisciplined High School Students," *Manas,* 19 (1972), 23–29.

Stebbins, Robert A. "Physical Context Influences on Behavior: The Case of Classroom Disorderliness," *Environment and Behavior,* 5 (1973), 291–314.

Stebbins, Robert A. "The Meaning of Disorderly Behavior—Teacher Definitions of a Classroom Situation," *Sociology of Education*, 44 (1971), 217–236.

Stevens-Long, Judith. "The Effect of Behavioral Context on Some Aspects of Adult Disciplinary Practice and Affect," *Child Development*, 44 (1973), 476–484.

Stiavelli, Richard E., and Dudley E. Sykes. "The Guidance Clinic—An Alternative to Suspension," *NASSP Bulletin,* 56 (1972), 64–72.

Sulzer, B., G. R. Mayer, and J. J. Cody. "Assisting Teachers with Managing Classroom Behavioral Problems," *Elementary School Guidance and Counseling,* 3 (1968), 40–48.

Swap, Susan M. "An Ecological Study of Disruptive Encounters Between Pupils and Teachers," *Proceedings of the 81st Annual Convention of the American Psychological Association*, 8 (1973), 521–522.

Thomas, D. R., W. C. Becker, and M. Armstrong. "Production and Elimination of Disruptive Classroom Behavior by Systematically Varying Teacher's Behavior," *Journal of Applied Behavior Analysis*, 1 (1968), 35–45.

Thurston, J. E., J. F. Feldhusen, and J. J. Benning. *Classroom Behavior: Background Factors and Psychosocial Correlates*. Madison, Wisconsin: State Department of Public Welfare, 1964.

Vitro, Frank T. "The Relationship of Classroom Dishonesty to Perceived Parental Discipline," *Journal of College Student Personnel,* 12 (1971), 427–429.

Wagner, Rudolph F., and Barbara P. Guyer. "Maintenance of Discipline Through Increasing Children's Span of Attending by Means of a Token Economy," *Psychology in the Schools*, 8 (1971), 282–289.

Ward, J. "Modification of Deviant Classroom Behaviour," *British Journal of Educational Psychology*, 41 (1971), 304–313.

Webb, A. Bert, and William H. Cormier. "Improving Classroom Behavior and Achievement," *Journal of Experimental Education*, 41 (1972), 92–96.

Wood, Frank H. "Negotiation and Justification: An Intervention Model," *Exceptional Children*, 40 (1973), 185–190.

Index

Index

Abrasive punishment, 24, 33
Acceptable alternatives, 26
Accountability, student, 8
Alertness, student, 7-8
   and mass-unison responses, 7
   and presentation of unusual
      material, 8
   and random recitation, 7
   and responses to mistakes, 8
   and skill demonstration, 8
   and suspense, 7
Alerts, practice, 12
Aronfreed, J., 29

Behavior modification, 19-22, 24-25
   constructive modeling, 20
   cueing, 21-22
   extinction principle, 20
   negative reinforcement, 21
   and self-control, 27
   token economy, 21-22
Behavioral programming, 28

Cause and effect explanations, 13
Check list, disciplinary technique
   evaluation, 35-37
Clarity, 16, 31, 32
Classroom meetings, 33
Commitment, 33

Consistency, 33
   of punishment, 25
   and rule breaking, 31
Control techniques
   exemplary, 11
   rough, 16
Corporal punishment, 23
Cueing, *see* Behavior modification

Daily schedule, 6
Dangle, 6
Deprivative punishment, 22, 25
Discipline, basic elements of good, 31

Environmental planning, 28
   see also Temptation removal
Extinction principle, *see* Behavior
   modification

Firmness, 16
Flip-flop, 6
Fragmentation
   group, 7
   prop or actone, 7
Force, physical, 13
Frustration, reducing, 11-12

Glasser's Reality Therapy, 30-33
Gnagey, W. J., 17-18, 24

Hurdle help, 12

Interest recharging, 13

Kounin, J. S., 5-10, 15-16

Laugh therapy, 12
Learning games, 9, 12
Lesson momentum, management errors in, *see* Fragmentation, Overdwelling
Lesson variety
　in content, 8
　covert behavior mode, 8
　group configuration, 9
　and learning props, 9
　location of activities, 9
　overt behavior mode, 9
　in presentation patterns, 9
　and student responsibility, 9

Mahoney, M. J., 27-28
Making an example, 16
Modeling
　constructive, 20
　and ripple effect, 20
　in token economy, 22
Motives, activating student, 12-13

Negative reinforcement, *see* Behavior modification

Optimal movement, 6
Overdwelling
　actone, 7
　behavior, 6-7
　prop, 7
　task, 7
Overlapping situations, 10

Positive reinforcement, *see* Behavior modification
Protective restraint, 13
Punishment
　effective use of, 24-26
　ineffective use of, 23-24
　and self-control, 29
　timing of, 29

Reality therapy
　illustration of, 30
　steps in using, 32-33
Redl, F., 12, 28
Revenge, *see* Punishment, ineffective use of
Rewards, 20, 26
　self-reward, 28
Ripple effect, 15-16, 31
　and influence of deviant's prestige on, 18
　and influence of deviant's response on, 18
Routines, 12
Rules, 33-34
　as cues, 21
　as element of discipline, 31

Self-control
　defined, 27-28
　learning of, 28
　punishment and, 29
　and self-management, 27
　as self-observation, 28
　teaching of, 28-29
Situation restructuring, 12
Slowdowns
　and frustration, 11
　in lesson momentum, 6-7
Smoothness, 5-7
Stimulus-boundedness, 6

Task-centered control techniques, 16, 31, 32
Temptation removal, 12
Thoreson, C. E., 27-28
Thrust, 6
Token economy, *see* Behavior modification
Transitions, 5-6
Truncation, 6

Variety, *see* Lesson variety
Visual signals, 12-13

Wattenberg, W., 12
Wineman, D., 12, 28
"Withitness," 9-10